# PET PROJECTS
## FOR YOUR
### CAT

# Pet Projects for Your Cat

Meow!

## Mary-Anne Danaher

TIME
LIFE
BOOKS

# CONTENTS

# INTRODUCTION

In a purr-fect world your cat would demand access to your lap and your complete attention at all times. While this may not always be possible, our little book of great ideas offers inspirational ways to spoil your kitty, so you can show just how much you care.

*Pet Projects for Your Cat* is a collection of beautiful projects to make for your beloved cat, whether it dreams of gourmet food, feathered toys to play with or a quiet and cosy place to curl up, there's something to suit all breeds and personalities.

Bring a little luxury, style and lots of fun into your cat's life with this invaluable book of creative ideas. The step-by-step photographs will have you making and finishing our easy projects in no time.

With chapters on everything from making cute collars and coats to massage, travel tips and delicious food, *Pet Projects for Your Cat* is sure to become one of your favorite references.

All the projects in this book have been tried and tested by cats and kittens and carry a unanimous seal of approval. *Meow! Meow!*

gorgeous bowls

yummy

fun and
games

7

dinnertime

get comfortable

# AT HOME

Cats love their homes and our beautiful soft furnishings are designed to bring extra comfort and a touch of luxury to their abodes. Our innovative ideas for housing will give your kitty many opportunities to sneak away and enjoy undisturbed slumber and privacy. There are also great dinner accessories and items for the holiday season.

# HOME COMFORTS

**Let your cat indulge in a little luxury every time it sinks into slumber with our beautiful ideas for soft furnishings.**

## Lined Cat Basket

Make or purchase a striped cushion to fit your kitty's basket. Personalize the cushion by painting your cat's name or KITTY on one of the corners using fabric paint, and follow the manufacturer's instructions to ensure that the paint sets properly.

To line the basket you will need a base piece and a side strip. Trace the bottom of the basket onto fabric and cut out this base piece, allowing 1in (2.5cm) extra all around. Cut a side strip of fabric two times the circumference of the basket for the length and two times the side measurement of the basket for the width. Pin and stitch the two short edges of this strip together, with right sides facing, then trim and neaten this seam.

Fold under and stitch a hem along one long edge of this piece, then work two rows of gathering stitches along the other edge. Pin the gathered edge to the outside edge of the base, with right sides facing, adjusting the gathers to fit. Stitch, trim and neaten the seam. Place the lining in the basket, fold the strip over to the outside and mark a line for attaching the elastic to secure the lining in place. Pin and stitch elastic along this line to complete the lining.

bed rest

10

# Knitted Cat Cushion

This gorgeous, generously sized
cushion is sure to become a favorite
place for your kitty to curl up. It is
decorated with a knitted paw-print
trail and MEOW, MEOW design.

comfort
zone

The knitting instructions for this colorful
cushion are in the Templates and Patterns
section on page 74.

# HOME COMFORTS

## Regal Sleeping Pillow

**Materials:** *20in (50cm) velvet fabric; small amount gold lamé fabric; cotton thread; foam beads; 12 gold bells.*

sweet dreams

1 Cut two 18in (45cm) square pieces of velvet for the cushion. Trace the crown template from the Templates and Patterns section on page 78, then cut two crowns from lamé. Pin gold crowns together at the center of the cushion top and use the satin or zigzag stitch on your machine to secure them in place.

2 With right sides facing, stitch the cushion pieces together around all the edges leaving a 2in (5cm) opening on one side. Trim and neaten the seams, turn the cushion right side out and fill it with foam beads. Hand-stitch bells onto the edge of the cushion, spacing them at even intervals.

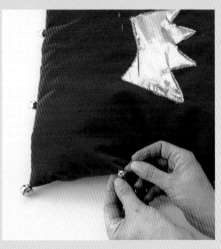

Utter luxury for the totally indulged cat—make this cushion and treat your kitty like royalty.

# HOME COMFORTS

## Shiny Throw Rug

**Materials:** *40in (1m) silk fabric;
32in (80cm) contrasting silk fabric;
silk thread; four gold tassels.*

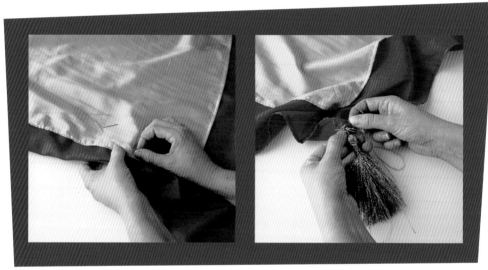

1 Cut a 40in (1m) square piece of main fabric and a 32in (80cm) square piece of contrasting fabric. Turn under and stitch a narrow hem around all edges of both pieces. Lay the main fabric square on a table or other sturdy flat surface and place the smaller square piece of contrasting fabric on top. Center this square, then pin and stitch it in place.

2 Pin and hand-stitch a tassel to each corner of the rug, twisting the ends of the tassels around to form decorative loops.

utter luxury

A soft and silky rug has tassels trimming the corners to entice your cat to play after a long rest.

# CAT ACCOMMODATIONS

**Every cat needs a quiet, safe and comfortable place to curl up when the action is over for the day—kittens, especially, need a place to crash when tired from playtime. Our innovative housing is designed with style and comfort in mind.**

## Cat Cabana

1. Paint the outside of the box and one side of the sheet of cardboard (which forms the facade) white, allow the paint to dry and apply another coat of paint. With a pencil, mark an opening in the center front bottom edge of the box, about 8in (20cm) x 6½in (15cm) and cut along these lines.

  Place facade and the front of the box together, center facade and trace around the hole in the box onto the back of the facade.

2. Place the facade on a firm surface, score along the two vertical lines that you've marked and cut along the horizontal line, then make a vertical cut in the center of the two vertical lines to form two doors. Carefully fold the two doors outward.

  Paint decorative details on the front of the facade and the sides of the box. Use our Moorish-inspired design or one of your own. When the paint is completely dry, apply one or two coats of varnish.

  Assemble the box and attach the cardboard facade to the front of the box with hot glue, first making sure the hole and the doors are aligned.

**Materials:** *Cardboard box; large sheet of cardboard (slightly larger all around than the widest side of the box); white and blue acrylic paint; craft knife; acrylic varnish; hot-glue gun and glue sticks.*

Your cat will love
hanging out in this house that
provides an escape from the world.
You can also make your own removable base for the home by
covering a sheet of heavy cardboard with felt or fur fabric,
then placing the house on top.

# CAT ACCOMMODATIONS

## Cat Cabana

**Materials:** *20in (50cm) heavy-duty waterproof nylon fabric; 12in (30cm) piece of dowel, ½in (1.25cm) in diameter; small length of rope; glue gun and glue sticks; metal grommet-fastener kit; narrow rope; tent pegs or metal staples.*

1 Cut a 20in (50cm) square of heavy-duty waterproof nylon fabric and find the center. Cut a hole big enough to fit the dowel through and glue the fabric in place around the dowel at this point, about 2in (5cm) from the top. Bind over the joint where you have just glued and to the top of the dowel with rope, securing it in place at intervals with hot glue.

2 Attach grommets at even intervals around the base of the cabana following the manufacturer's instructions. Cut and tie pieces of rope through these holes and secure it in the ground with tent pegs or metal staples. You will need to hammer the dowel into the ground so the cabana remains upright, then peg out the edges of the cabana to allow room inside it.

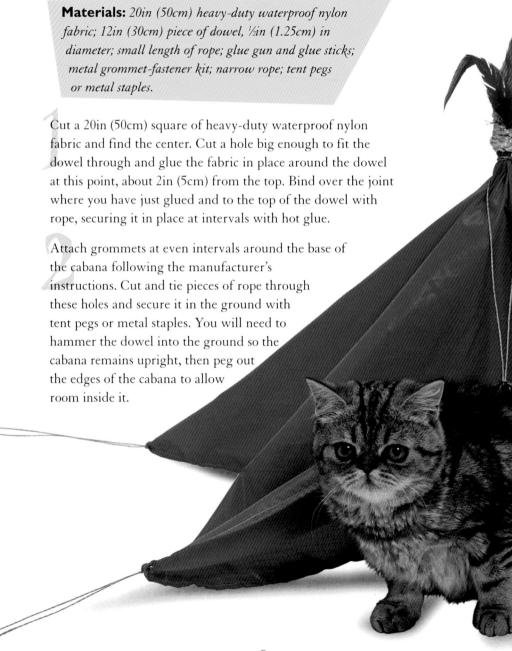

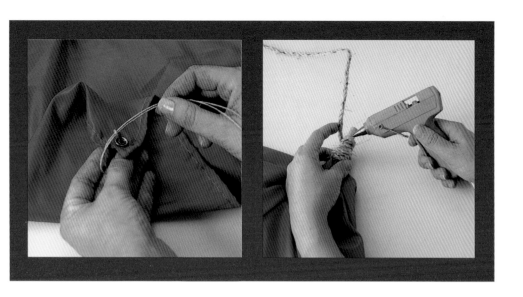

Your cat will want to slumber
away the hours inside this cute
tepee-style house that can be
used indoors or outdoors.

p e e k a b o o !

# HOME ACCESSORIES

**Our wonderful bowls will ensure that dinnertime is always a special occasion for your cat.**

## Stenciled Bowl and Feeding Mat

Use a purchased stencil to transform a plain plastic bowl and fabric mat into charming accessories for your cat. Choose a nontoxic multipurpose acrylic paint that is suitable for use on plastic and work the chosen stencil design on the base of the bowl and around the edge. Highlight the motifs by painting a narrow outline with a fine brush and a contrasting paint color. When dry, apply one or two coats of nontoxic sealer to the bowl to protect your design.

gorgeous!

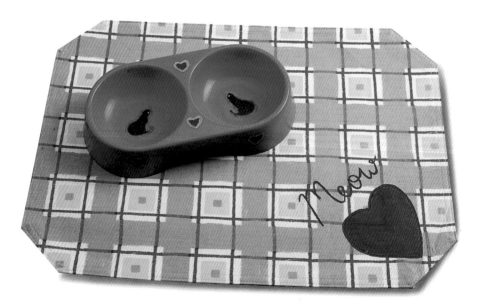

20

## Painted Ceramic Bowl

Use a nontoxic air-
drying ceramic or multi-
purpose paint that is
suitable for use on china and
ceramics to decorate a plain
bowl. Paint a simple fish motif
around the inside rim of the bowl and
then highlight the edge by painting a fine
line around the bowl. Allow the paint to cure,
then apply one or two coats of varnish or
sealer over the bowl, if desired.

# HOME ACCESSORIES

## Fancy Feeding Bowl

**Materials:** *Cat bowl; length of elasticized sequins (long enough to fit around the bowl); glue gun and glue sticks; assorted plastic jewels.*

**1** Secure the strip of sequins around the base of the bowl using hot glue. Overlap the ends at the back and fold under any raw edges to create a neat finish.

**2** Glue jewels onto the bowl to create your own design by mixing colors and alternating shapes.

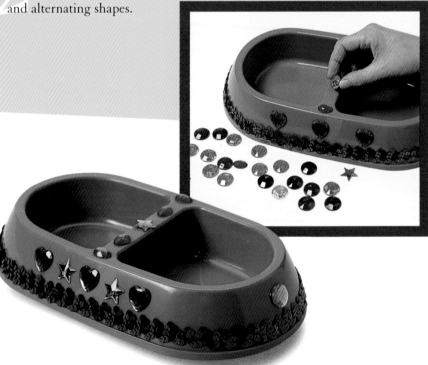

treasure
trove

A bejeweled bowl is the
perfect accessory for the
cat that you adore.

# THE FESTIVE SEASON FOR KITTY

**Make your cat feel part of the holidays with a great paw-print stocking to hang by the tree and an Advent calendar to count down the days to Christmas.**

## Paw Christmas Stocking

A paw-print stocking will ensure that your cat gets plenty of attention (and gifts) this Christmas. Trace the cat stocking pattern from the Templates and Patterns section on page 76 and enlarge as desired.

Cut two paw pieces from red felt and stitch them together around the edges, leaving the straight edge open.

Cut two strips of white felt for the trim and stitch them together along the short edges. Pin one long edge around the inside top of the stocking, stitch along this seam and fold over the white felt to the outside of the stocking. Attach a loop of ribbon for hanging the stocking.

season's greetings

24

# Cat Advent Calendar

**Materials:** *Rectangular cardboard box; sheet of cardboard (slightly larger all around than the top of the box); Christmas paper and cards; craft glue; felt-tipped pen; pencil; ruler; craft knife; ribbon; cat treats.*

1 Make a Christmas collage on the cardboard sheet by gluing different colored and patterned pieces of paper and card onto the cardboard. Rule lines to form boxes for the days from December 1 to 25 and fill in the numbers. Decide which days are to have treats behind them and cut along three sides of these boxes to form doors.

2 Place this collage sheet over the top of the box and using a pencil, make small marks on the inside of the box to indicate where the treats are to be positioned. Secure the treats in place with a little glue or restickable adhesive. Fold under the edges of the collage sheet and glue along these edges. Slip this sheet inside the box so the collage sheet sits flush with the top of the box. Decorate the outside of the box with ribbon by tying a large bow and securing it to the top and sides of the box with hot glue.

Your kitty will enjoy counting down the days and finding the treats behind the windows of this colorful calendar.

Even full-grown cats will be enticed to play with our cute and cuddly toys, including a furry mouse, a feathered friend and a catnip-filled rattle. Senior cats will love looking at the world from a different, higher perspective, on the top of our climbing platform. There's also an easy-to-make scratching pole that's guaranteed to keep kitty busy for hours.

# FOR PLAY

enticing toys

# ACTIVE CAT

**Planning activities for your cat need not be a problem with these great ideas for furniture and toys.**

## Climbing Platform

Cut a square piece of wood for the base, approx 40in (1m) x 24in (60cm). Cut four wooden plugs to fit the internal diameter of the pipe and cut two wooden platform tops. (Use thicker wood for the plugs.) Glue or nail two plugs to the base piece, spacing them as desired. Glue or nail a plug in the center of each platform top. Drill corresponding screw holes in the plugs and the pipe.

Cut a piece of fur fabric to cover the base, cutting holes for the plugs to fit through and secure it in place with double-sided tape or glue.

Cover each of the platform tops with foam before covering them with fabric to make a more comfortable resting place for your cat. Use glue or double-sided tape to secure the foam and fabric. Attach the pipe stands to the base plugs by screwing them together.

Cover the pipe stands with rope, and for an interesting effect, combine two or more colors of rope. Secure the rope at one end of the pipe with glue, then wind the rope around the pipe, securing it in place at intervals with glue. Leave the screw holes exposed at the tops of the pipe.

Place a platform top on each pipe stand and screw them together.

Place your climbing platform near a window or hang a number of toys from the highest platform to make it an interactive toy.

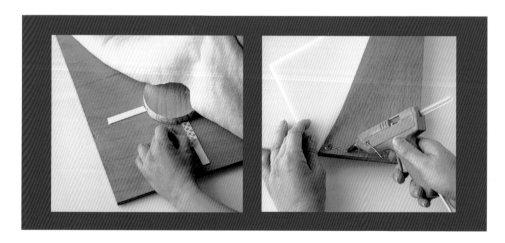

All cats love to climb, and when this comfortable platform is placed near a window, they can gaze out and watch the world go by too.

**Materials:** *Pieces of plywood for base, plugs and platform tops; two different lengths of PVC pipe for stands; glue gun and glue sticks, or nails; fake-fur fabric; double-sided tape; foam; screws; rope (to cover the pipe stands).*

# ACTIVE CAT

## Scratching Post

**Materials:** *Small pieces of lumber for base and plugs; piece of PVC pipe; glue gun and glue sticks, or nails; screws; fake-fur fabric; double-sided tape; carpet remnant; household staple gun*

s c r - r - r a t c h !

The perfect alternative to your home's best furniture—your cat can scratch away to its heart's content with our scratching post.

**1** Cut a thick piece of wood for the base, then make two wooden plugs to fit the internal diameter of the pipe. Glue or nail one plug to the center of the base. Cut out a piece of fur fabric to cover the base, cutting a hole for the plug to fit through, and use double-sided tape or glue to secure it in place.

**2** Make screw holes in the base plug and pipe so the holes correspond and secure the pipe to the base. (To increase the weight of the scratching pole, fill the pole section with sand before gluing the top plug in position.) Glue or staple the other plug in place at the top of the pipe to complete the pole. Cover the pole with carpet using double-sided tape, glue or staples to secure it in place. Cut a piece of carpet to cover the top of the pole and glue it in place.

# ACTIVE CAT
## Felt Fish Mobile

**Materials:** *Felt scraps, in a number of different colors; polyester toy filling; embroidery floss in contrasting colors to the felt; narrow elastic; 2 x 12in (30cm) pieces of dowel; glue gun and glue sticks.*

Great fun for kittens cats alike, our felt fis mobile is guarantee keep them amused for hours.

1 Draw a fish pattern and cut out the desired number of fish, remembering to cut two pieces for every fish. Place a small ball of filling between two matching fish pieces, then stitch together around the edges with running stitches (see Template and Patterns on page 78), using embroidery floss.

2 Stitch a length of elastic to the top of each fish, cutting the elastic different lengths to create the best effect for the mobile. You may want to join two fish with elastic to form double hanging fish.

Place the dowel pieces at right angles to each other and glue together at this center joint. Bind joint with a strip of felt, then cut long narrow strips of felt and twist and glue them around the dowel to form a spiral effect.

Tie the fish onto the ends of the dowel and secure them with a little hot glue.

Attach a length of ribbon or elastic to the top of the mobile for hanging or holding.

# TOYS

**All kittens love to play and many cats still like a game once in a while when they are full-grown. There's something to please all cats in our great range of handmade toys.**

*jingle all the way*

## Jingle Ball String

Tie a number of metal or plastic cat balls together with strands of braided ribbon to create this long string. Choose toys that have bells inside and allow extra ribbon at each end to entice your cat.

# Pom-Pom Bird

Glue a number of different-colored, medium-sized pom-poms together
to form the bird's body and head, then glue on feathers at the sides and
back to form wings and a tail. Attach a loop of narrow elastic to the
center back of the bird for hanging or holding, then bend a small
scrap of pipe cleaner in half and glue it to the bird's face to form
a beak. Hold the elastic loop and make the bird jump up and
down to encourage your kitty to play.

# TOYS

## Mouse Toy

**1** Trace the mouse toy pattern from the Templates and Patterns section on page 78. Cut a mouse piece from fur fabric. With right sides facing, fold the fabric in half lengthwise so the edges meet and the fabric forms a cone shape. Pin and stitch along this seam, leaving the wide end of the cone open.

**Materials**: *10in (25cm) fake-fur fabric; polyester toy filling; cotton thread; small length of rope.*

**2** Turn right side out and cut a piece of fur fabric slightly larger all around than the opening. Fill the mouse with polyester filling, then hand-stitch the round piece over the end of the toy to completely close the opening. Tie a knot at one end of the rope and glue or stitch the other end to the center of the wide end of the mouse.

m e o w !

g o t c h a !

Make a mouse toy using one of the many fake-fur fabrics available and don't forget to tie a knot at the end of its rope tail to attract your kitty's attention.

# TOYS

## Hanging Spider

**Materials:** *4 large pipe cleaners; 3 large pom-poms; craft glue; narrow elastic; sequins or beads, for eyes.*

c r e e p y    c r a w l y

1 Hold the pipe cleaners together at the center and twist one of them around the other three a couple of times at the center of the lengths to secure them together. Fan out the pipe cleaners and bend them all about 2in (5cm) from the end to form the spider's legs.

2 Glue the three pom-poms together to form the spider's body and allow the glue to dry. Glue the body to the legs and allow to dry, then attach a loop of elastic to hang the spider and glue the eyes in place.

Our creepy spider will keep your cat enthralled for hours and can be suspended from a chair or bench so your cat can stretch or jump for the toy.

# Sock Ball Toy

Simply recycle an odd sock for this project. Place a tennis ball inside the sock, then cut scraps of felt and glue or stitch these onto the toe of the sock to create a face.

# TOYS

## Catnip Rattle

**Materials:** *Film container; metal skewer or nail; dried catnip; 3 bells; small amounts of adhesive felt in two colors.*

1 Using a nail or skewer, make a number of holes in the body of the film container. Fill the container with dried catnip and place the bells inside before replacing the lid.

2 Cut a strip of felt to cover the body of the container and circles of the contrasting colored felt to cover the ends. Cut other decorations from the contrasting colored felt and stick these on the body of the container.

rattle 'n' roll

Simple to make and always popular with kitties, this rattle toy also has catnip inside to make your cat fall in love with it.

fancy florals

stunning!

# TO WEAR

We've got cat fashion all wrapped up with our selection of beautiful accessories. From a cotton cat coat that can be lined to provide extra warmth on cool days to our cozy fur wrap, your cat will be protected from the elements. Our selection of exquisitely decorated collars includes bejeweled models, one featuring a painted Egyptian motif and a frivolous pearl and lace combination.

# COVERUPS

**Our cool collars and ideas for covering up on chilly days will ensure your cat keeps abreast of the latest fashions.**

## Cotton Coat

**Materials:** *16in (40cm) cotton fabric; bias binding; cotton thread; Velcro or snaps.*

*1* Trace cat coat pattern from the Templates and Patterns section on page 79, enlarging or reducing the size to fit your cat. Cut out two coat pieces from fabric, place these with wrong sides together and pin around all the edges.

*2* Pin one side of the bias binding around these edges and machine stitch in place, fold the binding over the raw edges and hand-stitch the other side to secure by working invisible hem stitches.

Our cute cotton coat can be made with or without lining to suit the climate.

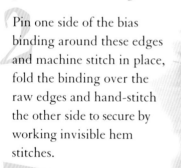

# Cat Wrap

A warm, furry wrap is perfect to snuggle into in cool weather and is quick and easy to make. Just cut a 10in (25cm) x 6in (15cm) piece of fake-fur fabric and fold it in half with right sides facing. Stitch around three sides leaving a 2in (5cm) opening. Trim and neaten the seams, turn the fabric right side out and hand-stitch the opening closed. Place it around your cat's neck to mark where the Velcro or snaps are to be placed, then stitch or glue them in place.

# COLLARS

**We've got great ideas for gorgeous collars no matter what the occasion.**

exotic eyelines

## Egyptian Collar

The eye design was favored by the Egyptians and featured in many of their paintings. Re-create this design on a leather collar using acrylic paints. When dry, seal with one or two coats of varnish.

## Diamonds are a Girl's Best Friend

Create this sparkling collar in just a few minutes. Attach clear, colored plastic stones onto a webbed collar using hot glue to secure them and voila! The collar is ready to wear.

diamond dazzler

## Stone-Encrusted Collar

This simple and elegant collar features colored stones and golden beads. Attach the stones to the collar with a hot-glue gun, leaving enough space between the stones for two golden beads; then glue on the beads.

kitty jewels

# COLLARS

## Floral Tribute Collar

Decorate a plain collar with silk or artificial flowers to create a band of flora around your kitty's neck. Simply cut individual flowers with very short stems and glue them in place on the collar using a hot-glue gun. Overlap the flowers slightly to cover any gaps.

# Pearl and Lace Fantasy

Give your kitty a glamorous new collar made by combining pretty lace with subtle pearls.

**Materials**: *Collar; 20in (50cm) lace or broderie anglaise; glue gun and glue sticks; pearls, in assorted sizes and shapes.*

1 Cut a strip of lace for each side of the collar, on the back of the collar apply glue along one edge and press the straight edge of the lace along this strip. Repeat with the other strip.

2 Turn the collar to the right side and glue the pearls along the center of the collar to form a pattern.

## Painted Glitter Collar

A glittering kitty collar is decorated using dimensional glitter paints. Paint words, such as KITTY, and hearts, dots or other motifs to create your own original design.

m-m-m-m d e l i c i o u s !

# MEALTIME

Introduce some gourmet food to
your cat's diet. Our healthy,
nutritious meals and snacks can
be served as an alternative
to commercial food or as a treat
on special occasions. If your cat
is overweight, consult your vet for
the best feeding and diet advice.
Once you start cooking meals for
your cat, you'll find just how easy
it is—and kitty is certain
to approve too!

# MAIN COURSE

**Make these mouthwatering meals and treats for your cat.**

## Tuna Cattuchini

*fresh egg noodle fettucine*
*1 teaspoon olive oil*
*7oz (220g) can tuna, drained*
*2 tablespoons cottage cheese*
*1 hard-boiled egg, chopped*

1 Cook fettucine following instructions on package and allow to cool.

2 Heat pan, add oil and tuna and stir for 2 minutes. Add cottage cheese and cook for 2 minutes.

3 Remove from heat, gently stir in egg and allow mixture to cool until just warm.

4 Combine mixture and fettucine and serve.

C a t t u c h i n i

## KitKat Maryland

*6oz (200g) chicken breast,*
*  cut into 2in (5cm) pieces*
*1 egg, lightly beaten*
*3½oz (100g) breadcrumbs*
*¾oz (20g) cheddar cheese, grated*

1 Dip chicken pieces into egg, then roll in combined breadcrumbs and cheese.

2 Heat pan, spray lightly with oil and add chicken pieces, cooking until they are just browned.

3 Remove from heat and allow to cool until just warm.

4 Serve on a bed of carrot sticks, if desired.

## Kitty Burgers

*10oz (315g) lean ground beef*
*1 medium carrot, grated*
*1 egg, lightly beaten*

1 Place all ingredients in a bowl and mix until combined, then form small amounts of mixture into mini-burgers.

2 Heat pan and lightly spray with oil. Place burgers in pan and fry until lightly browned.

3 Remove from pan, cool until just warm and serve.

B u r g e r s

## Fishysoisse

*10oz (315g) fish fillet, boned,*
  *chopped into 1½in (4cm) pieces*
*1 teaspoon olive oil*
*2 medium potatoes, diced*
*1 cup (235ml) chicken stock*
*2 cups (475ml) milk*

**1** Heat pan, add olive oil and potatoes and stir for 2 minutes.

**2** Add remaining ingredients and cook for 10 minutes. Remove fish pieces and set aside to cool.

**3** Blend or process mixture until smooth and allow to cool until just warm.

**4** Add fish pieces, stir gently and serve.

F i s h y s o i s s e

## Meal Times

🐱 Don't overcook the meat in the recipes. Just allow it to change color. Remove it from the pan during cooking then add it to the mixture just before serving.

🐱 These recipes can be served cold or just warm. Never overheat food. If using a microwave oven to heat food, heat it in small bursts until it reaches the desired temperature. The food should never be more than lukewarm and always cool enough for you to touch.

🐱 Add garnishes of raw vegetables such as carrots, beans and peppers when serving these recipes.

🐱 The recipes have been designed to make two servings but serve food as required according to your cat's size. If your cat is overweight, consult your vet before serving these recipes.

🐱 Introduce new foods slowly by adding a little more of a new food to each meal. You cat will soon begin to display its own taste and decide which recipes are to become favorites.

🐱 Give treats sparingly. Use them as a reward when training your cat or serve them on special occasions. They will also be great additions to kitty party bags or Christmas stockings.

🐱 Serve our delicious meals in one of the decorated bowls shown beginning on page 20 of the At Home chapter. Plain white oven-fired and air-dry china bowls and ceramic paints are available from good craft stores.

# TASTY TREATS

**Delectable little treats for when you want to show your cat how much you care.**

## Pussycat Paté

*16oz (500g) chicken livers*
*1/2tsp olive oil*
*1 1/2oz (45g) almond meal*
*1/2 bunch parsley, chopped*
*1 heaping tablespoon cottage cheese*

1 Heat pan, add livers and oil, and cook until lightly browned.

2 Add almond meal and parsley, and stir gently. Remove from heat and allow to cool for 10 minutes.

3 Stir in cottage cheese, then blend or process mixture until smooth.

4 Pour into baking tray or a number of small dishes or molds and refrigerate until firm.

5 Serve on toast or as a topping for a meal.

P a t é

## Kitty Latte Drink

*3fl oz (90ml) milk*
*1 egg*
*few drops of vanilla*
*cinnamon*

1 Combine milk and egg in a bowl and whisk until frothy.

2 Add vanilla and whisk lightly.

3 Pour into a bowl and sprinkle with cinnamon to serve.

L a t t e

54

# Herbed Biscuit Morsels

*1 cup white flour*
*¹/₂ cup (125ml) cheddar*
  *cheese, grated*
*4 tablespoons butter*
*¹/₂ cup (125ml) warm water*
*mixed herbs*
*1 egg, lightly beaten*

**1** Combine flour and cheese in a bowl and rub in butter. Mix well.

**2** Add water gradually to make a firm dough. Roll out onto a lightly floured surface and cut shapes using cookie cutters.

**3** Dip each biscuit into egg, then roll in mixed herbs to coat.

**4** Place biscuits on a lightly greased cookie sheet and bake in a moderate oven (375–400°F or 190–200°C) for 20 to 25 minutes or until lightly browned.

**5** Remove from oven. Cool and serve.

B i s c u i t s

# Liver Drops

*¹/₂ cup whole-wheat flour*
*¹/₂ cup white flour*
*¹/₃ cup butter, melted*
*1 egg, lightly beaten*
*¹/₄ cup dried liver pieces or liver jerky*
*¹/₂ cup (125ml) water*

**1** Combine flours, butter, egg and dried liver in a bowl and mix well.

**2** Gradually add enough water to make a firm dough. Make small rounds of mixture, place them on a lightly greased cookie sheet and bake in a moderate oven (375–400°F or 190–200°C) for 20 to 30 minutes or until lightly browned.

**3** Remove from oven. Cool and serve.

Purr-fect
Pampering

# PERSONAL HYGIENE

Treat your cat to the perfect pampering session by following our step-by-step instructions for grooming and massage. As well as the basics of brushing, we teach you how to massage your cat into a state of blissful contentment. There are also beautiful handmade grooming accessories for your own kitty or to give as gifts on birthdays and festive occasions.

# GROOMING

**Cats adore being petted and our step-by-step guide to massage and grooming techniques is the purr-fect way to treat a well-loved kitty.**

## Brushing

1 Brushing your cat will help remove dead hair and skin cells. Since cats are very proficient at cleaning themselves, you may only need to brush your kitty's coat once a week. Always follow the grain of the coat when brushing. For a gentle and soothing brushing of short-haired cats, use our grooming mitt, which will smooth their hair and can be used to give a minimassage.

2 Use a comb instead of a brush when removing tangles or any material that may have become caught in your cat's coat. Combs are also the perfect tool to use when grooming long-haired cats as you can get right to the ends of the hair to thoroughly clean the coat.

## Painted Comb Set

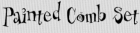

Use acrylic paints in the desired colors to work your designs on the brush and comb. You may like to copy our design or create your own. After the paint has dried, apply one or two coats of satin or gloss varnish on top of the paint to protect the surface.

## Grooming Mitt

Make your own grooming mitt from felt or flannel fabric. Just trace around your hand and thumb onto paper, cut out this pattern, then pin this onto doubled fabric and cut out two mitt pieces. Stitch these pieces together, close to the edge, using running stitches and embroidery floss. You can also stitch your cat's name or KITTY onto the front of the mitt to personalize it.

# MASSAGE

**Our three massage techniques are guaranteed to bring you and your cat even closer. Your cat's response to these methods will soon make you aware which is the best technique.**

1 A fingertip massage is a great way to begin a session, as it will quickly relax your cat. Using your fingertips and both hands, massage your cat's back, from the neck down, moving your fingers little by little. Then repeat this step but work in the opposite direction, against the hair and skin. Repeat the desired number of times.

2 Using only your thumbs and working each hand in the opposite direction, work small circular movements starting just below your cat's neck. As you massage down your cat's back, increase the size of the circular movements. Repeat again, beginning with large circular motions and working down to smaller motions.

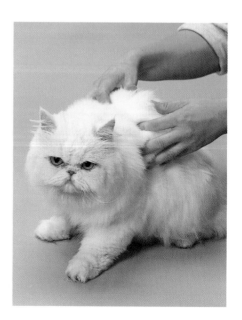

3 Begin by working small circles on your cat's chest, just under the head, using your thumbs, then when your cat is very relaxed, change your massage technique to use your fingertips, while working increasingly larger circular motions. Repeat two or three times.

partytime!

# PARTY ANIMALS

Make every one of your cat's birthdays a memorable event by celebrating it with a party. You may like to plan an intimate affair or invite family and friends to mark the occasion. Our ideas for making invitations and party bags and our instructions for great party games will ensure that your party's a hit. We've also included a number of helpful tips to make certain everything runs smoothly on the day.

# PARTY ANIMALS

**Our great ideas for food, fun and take-home treats will ensure that every cat party is a great success!**

## Kitty Treat Bags

Decorate brown paper to create your own unique take-home party bags. Make sure they're filled with great treats so all your family and friends will remember the event long after it's over.

Decorate the bags using markers, colored pencils, ink stamps and stickers. Write "KITTY BAG" on the front of the bags, then decorate them with freehand drawings of cat faces and paw prints.

Fill them with biscuits or tasty meat treats for the cats and other pets, or with sweet treats for human guests, then tie the bags up with ribbons and make sure every cat guest gets to take one home at the end of the party.

## Kitty Paw Prints

Create charming painted mementos for each animal guest and especially a record of the birthday cat's paw on this special day. Prepare a plate of paint and a number of sheets of cardboard. Dip each cat's paw into the paint and print it onto a card, then record their name, the date and the event for all time.

## Party Invitations

Make your own wonderful party invitations from colored cardboard.

Cut out rectangular, square or other shaped pieces of cardboard and fold them in half to make cards with a flap.

Use wrapping paper and colored cardboard to create the decorations on the invitations. Cut out a wrapping paper panel and glue it to the front of each card or cut a number of vertical and horizontal paper strips and glue them over each other to form a crisscross pattern.

You may also want to draw and cut out letters from contrasting colored cardboard to make words such as MEOW, PURR or CAT. Outline the letters with a marker, then glue them in position on the front of the card.

# Mouse Cake

*1½ lbs (750g) ground turkey or*
*chicken breast*
*1 egg*
*1 cup whole-wheat flour*
*½ cup white flour*
*1 chicken bouillion cube, crumbled*
*1 tablespoon cottage cheese*

**1** Combine turkey or chicken, egg, flours, bouillion cube in a bowl and mix well. Pour into a lightly greased cake pan or pudding mold and cook in a moderate oven (375–400°F or 190–200°C) for about 1 hour or until the cake is cooked through and comes away from the sides of the pan.

**2** Remove from oven and allow to sit for 5 minutes before turning the cake onto a rack to cool.

**3** Decorate the cake with cream cheese and tint with food coloring, if desired. Sprinkle with coconut, then decorate with marshmallows, jelly beans and licorice to create a mouse face. If you prefer, use savory treats to decorate the cake.

y u m m y !

## Party tips

❀ Plan to hold the party at your home where cats and any other pets will be comfortable with their surroundings.

❀ Limit the party to one hour as this will be as long as you can hold your cat's attention.

❀ Make and send out the invitations to family and friends and any special cat friends that may want to attend.

❀ Organize the catering. Make sure there is enough food for the animals and some for humans.

❀ Don't forget to take a photograph of the birthday cat.

bon voyage!

# ON VACATION

Take all the worry out of traveling with
accessories that will ensure a safe,
well-organized vacation. Our cute cat
travel box is for packing all the comforts
of home. As well as favorite treats, pack
a number of your cat's toys, so no matter
where you go, kitty will feel right at home.
Our cardboard car carrier is designed
to keep your cat restrained
on long car trips.

# ON VACATION

**The essentials for the feline on the move—our carrier and kitty carry case will ensure that holidays are a breeze.**

## Cardboard Car Carrier

Paint a medium-sized cardboard carton with colorful stripes and allow to dry. Mark rectangular air vents on the front, back and sides of the carton and cut out along these lines using a ruler as a guide and a craft knife. Cut pieces of tulle or net fabric slightly larger all around than the vents, then glue these in place on the inside of the carton.

Ideas for decorating the carrier include cutting out felt letters to spell out words, such as KITTY ON BOARD or your own phrase, and attaching them to the front of the box, or painting

wooden cat shapes and gluing these to the front of the carrier using a hot-glue gun.

Finally, make up the box and cut slits in two of the top flaps. (You may also want to line the inside floor of the box with a fur fabric or insert a rug for the journey.) When taking your cat in the car, tie these flaps together with string, ribbon or cord to keep the carrier securely fastened.

## Kitty Travel Case

**Materials:** *Papier-mâché or cardboard box; felt; ribbon; glue gun and glue sticks; cat-print fabric; adhesive felt letters; silk flowers.*

Trace around the lid of the box onto the felt, cut out this piece and glue it in place on the top of the lid. Glue the ribbon in place around the sides of the box lid.

Cut a strip of fabric to cover the sides of the box base and glue it in place, overlapping the ends to create a neat finish.

Draw the letters C, A and T on the felt backing paper, then peel them off and stick them on the lid. Cut single flowers with short stems and glue these around the edge of the box lid, overlapping the flowers slightly as you work. Attach a piece of ribbon for carrying the case, if desired.

## Tips for traveling

🐈 Make sure your cat wears identification that clearly displays its home address and the relevant contact numbers. Many cats have microchip implants, allowing them to be identified all over the country.

🐈 Never leave your cat locked in the car for long as the sun and heat will cause it to dehydrate very quickly.

🐈 If driving long distances, always stop every couple of hours to rest yourself and give your cat a chance to drink. If your cat is used to wearing a leash, take it out for a walk, but keep it on the leash at all times. There is no predicting what your cat will do in strange surroundings.

🐈 Speak with your vet for advice about sedating your cat, if necessary.

gift ideas!

# PRESENTS FOR CAT OWNERS

Purr-fect gifts for cat lovers—our
beautiful range of gift ideas can be
made quickly and easily and are
guaranteed to bring great delight
to every recipient. Our painted mug
and house plaque, and even the clay
decorated frame, can be personalized
to include the recipient's name,
the cat's name and a likeness
of the beloved kitty.

# PRESENTS FOR CAT OWNERS

**Every devoted cat owner will love these gifts, which are just made to treasure.**

## Cat House Plaque

**Materials:** *Lighweight cardboard; scissors; pencil; wooden plaque; acrylic paints; paintbrushes; wooden numbers.*

Draw or trace a cat shape onto cardboard. Cut out and trace around the outline to transfer it to both ends of the wooden plaque. Repeat with a heart motif, centering it at the base of the plaque.

Paint the motifs and allow them to dry, then outline the shapes in a contrasting color. Paint the edge of the plaque, using one or two colors, and allow to dry.

Paint the wooden numbers in the same color as the outlines and allow to dry, then glue them in position at the center top of the plaque. When the glue is dry, apply one or two coats of varnish over the plaque and allow to dry.

## Cat Mug

Using a non-toxic multi-purpose paint that is designed for use on china and ceramics, paint a colorful and quirky design on a plain coffee mug. Paint cat faces, words (such as MEOW) or patterns.

If designing the mug for a special recipient, include the pet's name and try to capture the cat's coloring in your design. When the paint is dry, apply one or two coats of acrylic varnish over the painted surface and follow the manufacturer's instructions for curing.

# Clay-decorated Frame

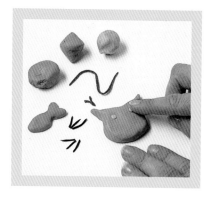

**Materials:** *Molding clay (in a variety of colors); baking tray; wooden picture frame; acrylic paints; paintbrush; craft glue; acrylic varnish.*

Warm the clay following the manufacturer's instructions. Choose one color for the cat's face and contrasting colors for the eyes, mouth, nose and whiskers and fish. Roll out and form the clay into the desired shapes, then assemble the decorations.

Place them on a baking tray and follow the manufacturer's instructions for baking. When baked, remove from the oven and allow to cool.

Paint the frame the desired color, applying two coats of paint and allowing drying time between each coat. You may wish to decorate the frame using two different colored paints. When the first coat dries, brush a lighter color on top to create a streaked effect. Use a brush with coarse bristles to achieve the best effect and apply the paint undiluted, a little at a time.

Secure the cat face and fish decorations to the frame using craft glue and allow to dry. Apply one or two coats of acrylic varnish, if desired. When the paint is dry, place your favorite photograph inside the frame.

This simply beautiful idea makes a wonderful gift for a cat-lover friend or is a great way to display photographs of your favorite kitty.

# TEMPLATES and PATTERNS

## Cat Cushion

**Materials:** 8-ply knitting yarn (50g balls). Main Color (M—gold): 10 balls; 1st Contrast (C1—navy): 3 balls; 2nd Contrast (C2—red): 1 ball. One pair No. 8 (4.00mm) knitting needles or size needed to give correct tension. Knitters needle for embroidery. 44in (110cm) Calico for Insert. Bean Bag Filling.

**Measurements:** Cushion measures approx 20in (50cm) x 20in (50cm).

**Tension:** 22 sts and 30 rows to 4in (10cm) over stocking st, using No. 8 (4.00mm) needles.

Please check your tension carefully before commencing. Wrong tension will result in a cushion that is the wrong shape or size.

**Abbreviations:** beg = beginning; cm = centimeters; dec = decrease; inc = increase, include or inclusive; rem = remain/ing; rep = repeat; st/s = stitch/es; stocking st = 1 row knit, 1 row purl.

## BACK AND FRONT OF CUSHION

Using No. 8 (4.00mm) needles and M, cast on 88 sts.

**1st row (wrong side):** Purl.
**2nd row:** Inc knitways in first st, knit to last st, inc knitways in last st.
**3rd row:** Inc purlways in first st, purl to last st, inc purlways in last st.
**4th row:** As 2nd row.
Rep rows 1 to 4 incl 3 times more.
Work a further 115 rows stocking st, beg with a purl row.

Dec at each end of next 3 rows.
Work 1 row.
Rep last 4 rows until 88 sts rem.
Work 1 row.
Cast off.

## GUSSET

Using No.8 (4.00mm) needles and M, cast on 19 sts.

Work in stocking st until gusset measures 76in (190cm) from beg, ending with a purl row.

Cast off.

## TO ASSEMBLE

With a slightly damp cloth and warm iron, press lightly on wrong side. Using Knitting Stitch, embroider motifs from Graph to front of Cushion as illustrated.

Using Back Stitch and C1, embroider around each letter, then using C2, embroider around center of paw print (as illustrated). Using back-stitch, join gusset seam. Pin gusset in position evenly around front of Cushion, placing seam on gusset to center of one side. Sew gusset in position, leaving a 1¼in (3cm) opening at gusset seam for twisted cords. Pin back of Cushion to other side of gusset in same manner and sew in position along 3 sides, leaving rem side open to insert Cushion Insert.

**For Cushion Insert.** Cut from Calico into 2 x 23in (52.5cm) squares for Back and Front of Insert and 2 strips each

4in (10cm) wide x 39in (98cm) long for gusset. Trim around corners of Back and Front of Cushion Insert pieces to form curves, beg at approx $2\frac{1}{2}$in (6cm) from each corner.

**Note:** $\frac{1}{4}$in (1cm) has been allowed on all sides of all pieces for seams. Machine stitch gusset pieces together along ends. Pin gusset evenly around Front of Cushion Insert and machine stitch in position. Pin Back of Cushion Insert to other side of gusset in same manner and machine sew around all edges, leaving a 4in (10cm) opening in one side for filling.

Turn insert through to right side and press well. Fill insert with bean bag filling (a large-necked funnel makes job easier) and sew up opening. Place cushion insert inside knitted cover. If required, place small amounts of dacron fiber filling around edges of insert to fill cover. Sew up remaining seam. Using 12 strands of C1, 240in (6m) long for each, make 2 twisted cords and pin in position around gusset, along seam lines as illustrated, noting to place ends of twisted cords inside openings left at gusset seam.

Sew twisted cords in position, noting to close openings at gusset seam neatly.

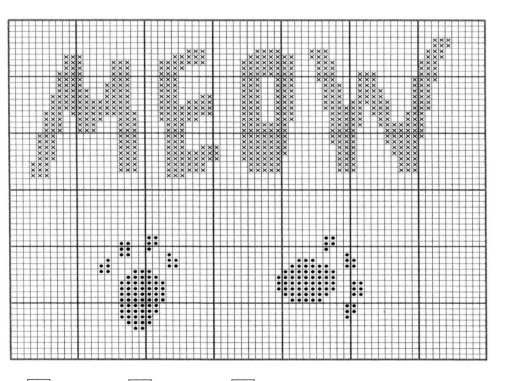

☐ = m     ● = C1     ☒ = C2

*Use a photocopier to enlarge or reduce templates and patterns as desired to fit your cat.*

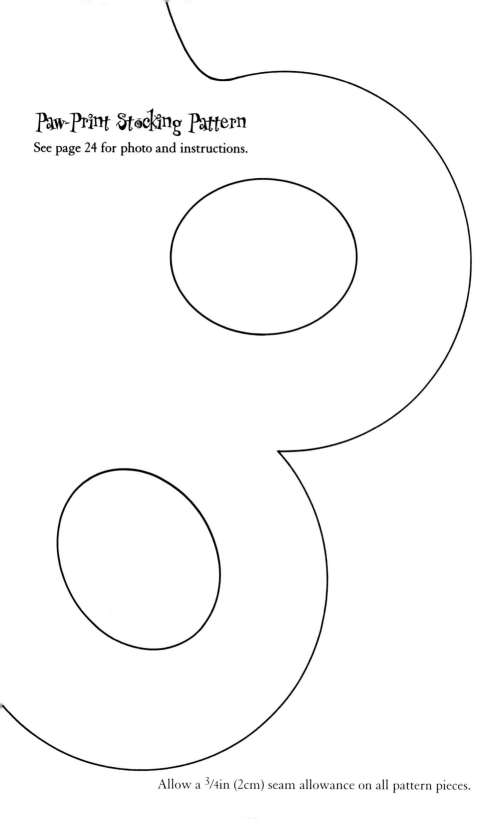

# Paw-Print Stocking Pattern
See page 24 for photo and instructions.

Allow a $3/4$in (2cm) seam allowance on all pattern pieces.

# TEMPLATES and PATTERNS

## Crown Template

(for regal sleeping pillow)
See page 12 for photo
and instructions.

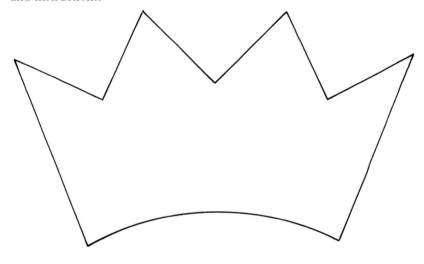

## Mouse Toy Pattern

See page 36 for photo and
instructions.

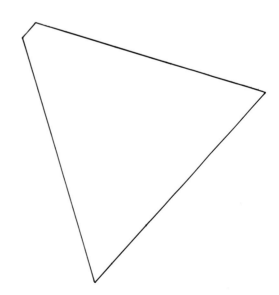

Allow a $3/4$ in (2cm) seam
allowance on all pattern pieces.

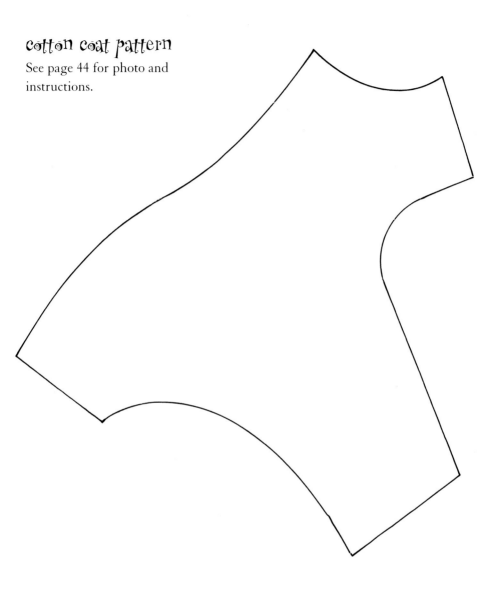

# cotton coat pattern

See page 44 for photo and
instructions.

*Use a photocopier to enlarge
or reduce templates and patterns
as desired to fit your cat.*

Time-Life Books is a division of Time Life Inc.
TIME LIFE INC. U.S.A.
President and CEO: George Artandi
Executive Vice President: Lawrence J. Marmon

TIME-LIFE CUSTOM PUBLISHING
Vice President and Publisher    Neil Levin
Director of Acquisitions and Editorial Resources   Jennifer Pearce
Editor    Linda Bellamy
Director of Creative Services    Laura McNeill
Technical Specialist    Monika Lynde

Produced by Lansdowne Publishing Pty Ltd
©1999 Lansdowne Publishing Pty Ltd
First published 1999

Library of Congress Cataloging in Publication Data
Danaher, Mary-Anne.
    Pet Projects for your cat:easy ways to pamper your kitty/by Mary-Anne Danaher
    p. cm.
Includes index.
ISBN 0-7370-0053-8 (softcover: alk.paper)
1. Cats--Equipment and supplies. 2. Handicraft. 3. Gifts.
I. Title
SF447.3.D25 1999            99-29322
636.8'0028'4--dc21           CIP

Printed in Hong Kong